ZEN COMICS (II)

Compiled and Drawn
by
IOANNA SALAJAN

CHARLES E. TUTTLE COMPANY
Rutland, Vermont   Tokyo, Japan

copyright 1982

Representatives

Continental Europe: Boxerbooks, Inc., *Zurich*
British Isles: Prentice-Hall International, Inc., *London*
Australasia: Book Wise (Australia) Pty. Ltd.
104–108 Sussex Street, Sydney 2000

Published by the Charles E. Tuttle Co., Inc. of Rutland, Vermont & Tokyo, Japan; with editorial offices at Suido 1-chome, 2-6, Bunkyo-ku, Tokyo. Copyright in Japan, 1982, by Ioanna Salajan. All rights reserved.

Library of Congress Catalog Card No. 82-50094. International Standard Book No. 0-8048 1445-7. Fourth printing, 1987   Printed in Japan.

for Tony

and with thanks to
Richard and Avistha

ZEN COMICS

ZEN COMICS

ZEN COMICS

Panel 1:
A reknowned scholar came to visit the old monk and discuss the precepts.

What is the meaning of the Buddhist teachings.

Panel 2:
Don't commit any evils. Practice the many virtues. Purify the mind.

Panel 3:
Oh, even a three year old child can say that!

Panel 4:
That may be but can you live it?

ZEN COMICS

Master, I've been reading about the stringless harp........

..... will you play it for me?

O.K., come and sit down.

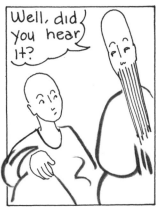

Zen Comics

It's not where you're going
It's how you're going

ZEN COMICS

ZEN COMICS

If the seer is a flower....

...the seen is a flower too.

ZEN COMICS

ZEN COMICS

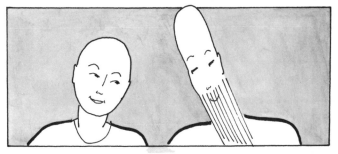

ZEN COMICS

ZEN COMICS

Zen Comics

SZENCOMICSZENCOMICSZEN

one who is pretending to
sleep cannot be awakened.

ZEN COMICS

ZEN COMICS

There, a perfect job!

ZEN COMICS

...and to stop my mind and form no wrong ideas.

I don't ask you to shut your eyes, but you don't see a thing.

I don't ask you to cover your ears, but you don't hear a sound.

I don't ask you to stop your mind, but you have no idea at all.

ZEN COMICS

ZEN COMICS

ZEN COMICS

Zen Comics

—36—

rice in the bowl.
water in the bucket.

Zen Comics

ZEN COMICS

Zen Comics

Zen Comics

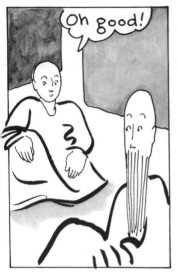 

Zen Comics
Zen Comics

eternity is the amount of time
it takes to know everything.

Master what is the best way to perfect the self?

Well, if I were planning things I would make an ideal environment for perfection of self.

What would you call that?

That? I think I'd call that living.

ZEN COMICS

ZEN COMICS

ZENCOMICSZENZENCOMICSZEN

Zen Comics

ZEN COMICS

Zen Comics

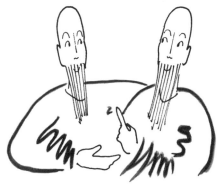

HOW ARE THINGS?   JUST AS THEY ARE.

ZEN COMICS

apart from
your self
there is no
Buddha

Zen Comics

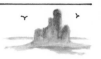

Master, how do I enter zen?

Do you hear the sound of that little mountain stream?

Yes, I do.

Enter zen from there.

Master, I've been thinking......what if I had said I couldn't hear the mountain stream...what would you have said then?

Disciple?

Yes master?

Enter zen from there.

when pure gold
enters the fire,
its colour becomes
still brighter.

Zen Comics

ZEN COMICS

a flower does not talk

ZEN COMICS

ZEN COMICS

ZEN COMICS

to lite a candle
is to cast a
shadow

ZEN COMICS

 # ZEN COMICS

Master, is the world really round?

Well yes and no.

satori
is
a state
of
Being

ZEN COMICS

Master, there is so much to know.

Disciple, once when I was studying......

..... some guests came to stay at our monastery.

Each one of them was enlightened.

ZEN COMICS

ZEN COMICS

Zen Comics

Zen Comics

ZEN COMICS

Master, is it true that you can see in the dark?

Yes, I can.

Then why are you carrying a lamp?

To keep other people from bumping into me!